Table of Contents

Introduction — 2

Lesson Activity Overview — 3

Lesson 1: What is Theatre?/Observation — 4

Lesson 2: Creating an Ensemble (1) — 7

Lesson 3: Creating an Ensemble (2) — 10

Lesson 4: Movement & Space (1) — 12

Lesson 5: Movement & Space (2) — 14

Lesson 6: "Where"/Environment (1) — 16

Lesson 7: "Where"/Environment (2) — 18

Lesson 8: "Who"/Character Development (1) — 20

Lesson 9: "Who"/Character Development (2) — 23

Lesson 10: "Why"/Objective & Tactics — 26

Lesson 11: Focus/Concentration — 28

Lesson 12: Utilizing Voice (1) — 30

Lesson 13: Utilizing Voice (2) — 33

Lesson 14: Listening/Reacting — 35

Lesson 15: Stage Directions/Blocking — 38

Lesson 16: Putting it All Together — 41

All lesson plans are designed for a 60-minute session for kids age 7-16. Level (1) is generally geared toward kids at the lower range of the 7-16 age spectrum, while Level (2) is geared toward kids at the higher range of the 7-16 age spectrum. Mixing and matching to best suit your students' abilities is absolutely encouraged. The lessons do not need to be followed in order.

Copyright © 2014 Beat by Beat Press. All Rights Reserved.
This eBook is meant for personal use only. Copying or distributing over the internet is prohibited by federal law.

Introduction

The goal of this eBook is to provide you with specific tools and lesson plans to help you develop the growth of the young actors in your drama program.

When I first started teaching theatre, I know the thing that was most helpful to me was to watch other teachers in action. I sat in with dozens of incredible teaching artists of all different styles absorbing every tool and technique I could. Sure I read all the books on theory and theatre education, but nothing could replace the experience of being in the classroom and seeing what worked and what didn't.

This eBook is designed to recreate that experience. After you've read through all the lessons, you should feel like you've sat in on an entire semester of observing an expert drama teacher introduce the basics of drama to a classroom of students. That's why these lessons are quite a bit more detailed that your typical lesson plan. It's up to you to choose how you want to implement the lessons. Feel free to try them out exactly as is, or adapt using your own toolbox you've developed over the years. As you progress you'll learn what works best with your specific group.

These 16 lessons represent what I think are the strongest (and most fun) ways to introduce kids to the art of acting.

About the Author

For nearly a decade **DENVER CASADO** has worked as an arts educator with New York City's leading theatre organizations including *Disney Theatricals*, *New York City Center* and *Young Audiences New York*. Denver's innovative approach to exploring theatre with kids has earned him invitations to speak at the national conferences of the *American Association of Community Theatre* and the *American Alliance for Theatre Education*. In 2011 he was honored with the  All Stars Projects' Phyllis Hyman award, in recognition of his important contribution to the creative growth and development of over 20,000 young people in the NYC public school system. Denver is a graduate of New York University's Steinhardt School of Education.

Lesson Activity Overview

Lesson 1
Stop, Go, Jump!
What is Theatre?
Mirror Activity
Quick Change
Slow Motion Emotion

Lesson 2
Toe to Toe
Walking Blind: Trust Exercise #1
Group Shape
The Machine

Lesson 3
One Word Story
Why An Ensemble Matters
Passed Around: Trust Exercise #3
Give and Take

Lesson 4
What is Pantomime?
Sound Ball
Bucket of Water
Tug-of-War

Lesson 5
3 Person Tableau
Ding!
Pantomime Scenes

Lesson 6
Environment Exploration
Birthday Party Environment
Three Objects

Lesson 7
Two Person Environment
Group Environment
Where Conversation

Lesson 8
Exaggeration Circle
Character Exploration
Bus Top
Status [option 1]
Hitchhiker [option 2]

Lesson 9
Human Barometer
Character Discussion
Facebook Profile
Character Improv

Lesson 10
Who wants a candy bar?
Objective/Tactics Exploration
Smile!
Create a Scene

Lesson 11
Group Count
Focus Exploration
Pass the Sound
"Sausage"
3-way Conversation

Lesson 12
Voice Exploration
Vocal Warm-Up
Vocal Exaggeration Circle
Tongue Twisters
Group Story with Characters

Lesson 13
Gibberish Introduction
Gibberish Interpreter
Gibberish Conversation

Lesson 14
Bippity Bippity Bop
Listening/Reacting Exploration
TV Reaction
The Phone Rings
Twin Interview

Lesson 15
Stage Directions
Principles of Blocking
Model a Tableau
Group Tableau

Lesson 16
Warm-Up of Choice
Observation Sheet Exploration
Scene Creation
Scene Sharing/Observation

Lesson 1: What is Theatre?/Observation

OBJECTIVE: Students will demonstrate the understanding that theatre is the art of telling stories through acting, and how observing the world around you is a first step to becoming a great actor.

MATERIALS:
- Large writing surface (dry erase board/chart paper)
- A bowl with slips of paper that have different emotions written on them (see list on page 7)

GREETING: Greet the students, introduce a little bit about yourself, then immediately begin the warm-up.

> I recommend beginning each session with a few words about what the goal/plan is for the day, then immediately jumping into a warm-up activity. Especially with young kids, it's important to get them moving and engaged as soon as possible.

WARM-UP: Drama Game: Stop, Go, Jump!
- Tell the students to take the stage. (From this point on "stage" will refer to any open playing area.)
- When you say *GO*, they are to walk around the stage trying to fill up all the space, not leaving any gaps.
- When you say *STOP* they should stop. Try this out a few times.
- When you say *CLAP* they should clap, when you say *JUMP* they should jump. Try this out a few times, then mix it in with *GO* and *STOP*.
- When you say *KNEES* they should bend over and put their hands on their knees, when you say *SKY* they should reach up toward the sky. Try this out, mixing it in with the previous commands.
- After they've gotten the hang of this, kick it up to Level 2. They are now to do everything in exact opposite. STOP means GO, GO means STOP, CLAP means JUMP, JUMP means CLAP, KNEES means SKY, SKY means KNEES.
- Try out this new level for awhile, slowly at first, then increasingly faster.
- Finally, kick it up to Level 3. You, the instructor, will be doing the actions literally as you say them, however the students should continue doing the exact opposite.
- Gather the students into a circle to reflect:
  - *Why do you think we played this game? What skills were we working on?*
  - *As an actor, you're going to be required to do things that sometimes feels unnatural, to step outside your comfort zone, and to always be focused and listening for direction. This helps prepare us for that.*

EXPLORATION: What is theatre? What makes a good actor?
- Ask the students if they can describe what theatre is.
  - How is it different than reading a book?
  - How is is different than watching a movie?

> Have the students seated for this next activity. The best time to have the students seated to explore a new concept or idea is immediately following the warm-up activity.

- *Theatre is the art of telling stories through live acting.*
- *We train to be good actors because we want to be the best we can at connecting with an audience to tell stories.*
- Draw a picture of a large stick figure on the board
- Ask the students to list what they think makes a good actor.
- As you receive suggestions, write them down with arrows pointing from the stick figure.
- Some of the suggestions you should receive:
    - Can play different characters, can speak loudly, works together well, funny, can take directions, doesn't goof off (focused), etc.
    - Add any items they missed.
- *Our work from here on out will be on exploring and developing the skills necessary to be a great actor; to best act out stories and connect with an audience.*

> Too often I feel like drama classes (or any classes, really) jump into lessons without taking a moment to explore why we're doing what we're doing. If every lesson stems from the central goal of "connecting with an audience to tell stories", it's much easier to stay focused and motivated when doing various activities, many of them very silly. If things ever get out of hand in the classroom, take a moment to pause and remind the students of what theatre is really all about.

ACTIVITY: Drama Game: The Mirror Activity

- *In order to play different characters and act out different situations we need to be aware of what's around us, and notice the details; Observation.*
- Pair the students up and have them assign one person as "A" and another as "B". Tell the pairs to face each other.
- When you say "action", A is to move very slowly, and B is to closely "reflect" every movement.
- Encourage the "reflection" to notice not only body movements, but facial expressions as well.
- After awhile have the partners switch.
- *The goal is to have an outside observer not be able to tell who is the leader and who is the follower.*
- Walk around the room and say you're going to choose two pairs who you think are the best "reflections".
- Have everyone sit and focus on these two pairs. Allow them to guess who is leading and who is following.
- For older groups, consider adding Mirror: 4 Person Variation.

> The "Mirror Activity" is so common in drama classes because it works. It's just as effective with 1st graders as it is with 8th graders.

> Consider playing calming, instrumental music after you say "Action" to enhance the focus and experience.

ACTIVITY: Drama Game: Quick Change

- Have the students seated in a circle.
- Choose one student to be the "changer". Let the class study his/her appearance for 1 second. Ask the "changer" to leave the room out of sight.

- While out of sight the "changer" must change three things about his/her appearance (pull a sock down, change watch from one wrist to another, unbutton a button, etc.)
- When the student enters, the class must figure out what three things changed.
- Continue this for several rounds.
- *We must train ourselves to notice the little things. These little things will add up to help us create unique characters.*

ACTIVITY: Drama Game: Slow Motion Emotion
- Ask three students to take the stage.
- Have the students draw an emotion from the bowl.
- As you slowly count down from 10 to 1, they are to gradually put that emotion in their bodies and their faces.
- Have the class guess which emotion they chose and reflect on what gave away that emotion.

REFLECTION:
- *What is theatre? Why are we trying to be better actors?*
- *Drama Journal*: This week, observe the people around you, family, friends, teachers, strangers. Choose one interesting person and write three sentences describing them in your journal.*

> *Before your classes begin, instruct every student to bring an empty notebook that will become their "drama journal". (Or provide one for them.) These will be used after every class to explore the content further. Encourage the students to use these notebooks however they feel inspired as your semester progresses. (I've had many students bring in full scenes they've written because they get excited about an idea :)*

List of emotions:
Angry
Sad
Embarrassed
Frustrated
Annoyed
Eager
Shy
Nervous
Loving
Confident
Proud
Curious
Fascinated
Excited
Energetic
Surprised
Grateful
Touched
Hopeful
Happy
Peaceful

Lesson 2: Creating an Ensemble (1)

OBJECTIVE: Students will learn to work together, build trust, and involve each member in group performance/activities.

MATERIALS: None.

GREETING: Reflect on previous session, ask students to share their journal entries, set up goal for today.

WARM-UP: Drama Game: Toe to Toe
- Instruct the students that when the music begins, they are to silently walk around the space. When the music stops, they are to freeze and listen for directions.
- Play music for about 20 seconds. Stop music.
- *Connect toe to toe with someone you don't know very well in 3...2...1! Introduce yourself to your toe partner and tell them what your favorite food is and why.*
- After about 30 seconds, play music again and the kids will start walking around. Encourage them to feel the music and put it into their bodies. Stop the music.
- *Connect elbow to elbow with a different partner in 3...2..1! Introduce yourself to your elbow partner and tell them your favorite teacher and why.*
- After about 30 seconds, play music again. Tell them to dance to it. Let them enjoy it. Stop the music.
- *Connect high-fives with a different partner in 3...2...1! Introduce yourself to your high-five partner and tell them your favorite part about acting and why.*
- After about 30 seconds, play the music again. Stop the music.
- *Connect with your original toe to toe partner, go!* Let them scramble. *Now staying connected with your toe partner, connect to your elbow partner!* Let them scramble. *Now staying connected with your toe and elbow partner, connect with your high-five partner!*
- By this time they should pretty much be in a messy human knot. After the chaos has reached it's peak, tell the kids to relax and go back to standing in a large circle. Take a couple deep breathes as a group to calm the energy.
- Ask for a volunteer to share one thing they learned about somebody in this group they didn't know before. Continue asking volunteers to share information they learned about their partners.

The music can be anything, but ideally each time you play a new track it will have a contrasting emotion. Consider playing the soundtrack to the musical you'll be rehearsing, or have your music director improvise, or just play your favorite songs from your phone/ipod.

Allowing the kids to share with just one other person first allows them to build their confidence in a way that might be intimidating in front of a whole group. By starting small, it creates an easy way for even shy kids to begin feeling comfortable.

The instructions you give for each "connection" where students tell their partner their interesting fact is completely up to you.

- Remind the students that over the next few weeks they will be working closely as an ensemble. The more connected they are, the more trust there is between actors, the better their performances will be.

ACTIVITY: Drama Game: Trust Exercise #1
- *Speaking of trust, let's explore that a little bit.*
- Divide the students up into partners.
- Partner A is instructed to close their eyes as Partner B *silently* leads them around the space. Partner B's goal is to make their partner feel as safe as possible.
- They must determine what is best for their partner (without talking) – walking with both hands held, one hand held, arm around shoulder, whatever works. Don't instruct them what to do, let them figure it out.
- Let them wander for 2 minutes or so, keeping their movement slow at all times. Consider playing some calming music. Switch partners, now Partner A will lead Partner B.
- *How did you make your partner feel safe? What did your partner do that made you feel safe?*

ACTIVITY: Drama Game: Group Shape
- Have the whole class take the stage.
- Tell them their goal is to create the shape of an object with their bodies as you count down from 10 to 1. When you reach "1" and say "freeze!" they must freeze as you inspect the object. (see object ideas to the right)
- The first couple times don't give them any instructions and let them try to figure it out however they want, even if it includes talking. You'll see a lot of personalities come out.
- Then, tell them they must work silently.
- After awhile, consider dividing the class up into two or three groups. Call out an object and have them compete to see who can create the best shape in 10 seconds.
- For more advanced groups:
    - Have each group create an object of their own while other groups guess.
    - Or, give them an object that has motion, and ask them to demonstrate the moving object (see list to the right)

> Object Ideas:
> - A plane
> - An iPhone
> - A piano
> - A shoe
> - A giraffe
> - A teepee
>
> Movement Objects:
> - Fire
> - A tree in a storm
> - An eagle
> - A blinking eye
> - A ticking clock
> - A wave
> - A train

ACTIVITY: Drama Game: The Machine
- *The goal of this game is for each actor to become part of a working machine.*
- Ask one student to take the stage and make a noise and a simple repeatable gesture.
- Ask another student to join the first students and make a new noise and movement that connects to the first actor.

- Continue until you have about 6 students as part of the machine, all with a unique sound and movement.
- Turn the machine "off" by pulling an imaginary giant lever. The machine should freeze.
- Ask a volunteer to take the stage, turn each individual part of the machine on, and describe its function ("This part of the machine mixes the dough, this part adds water, etc.")
- After each "individual" part has been explained, the volunteer can turn the giant lever on to bring the whole machine back to life. Then he/she should give it an official name.

REFLECTION:
- *Why is it important to work as an ensemble? What other activities are you involved in that requires work as an ensemble? Make a list of 3 of them in your journal.*

Lesson 3: Creating an Ensemble (2)

OBJECTIVE: Students will learn to seamlessly work together, support each other, and allow space so every member of the ensemble has an opportunity to contribute.

MATERIALS: [None]

GREETING: Reflect on previous lesson, share a few journal entries, layout the goal for today.

WARM-UP: Drama Game: One Word Story
- In a sitting circle, explain the rules of the game:
- One person says a single word to begin a story.
- The person to his/her left says another word, then the next person says another word, continuing around the circle.
- The goal to tell a coherent story, one word at a time.

> This is a challenging game at first. Any time the story gets off track, reset and start over. Consider also trying this out in two teams, competing in turns to see which team can go the longest keeping the story coherent.

DISCUSSION: Why An Ensemble Matters
- *Creating a play is just like telling a group story.*
- *Each person is an important part of the process.*
- *If one actor is not focused or contributing to the story it brings the whole piece down.*
- *The more comfortable each actor is, and the more trust he/she has in her fellow actors, the more successful the performance will be.*

ACTIVITY: Drama Game: Trust Exercise (#3)
- Choose 6-8 students to help you demonstrate the activity.
- Arrange the students in a close circle.
- Ask one volunteer to go to the middle, arms crossed over his/her chest. Ask the students in the circle to stand in a firm, balanced position (knees slightly bent, feet shoulder width apart and slightly staggered, hands up ready to catch).
- When the student is ready, they may slowly fall forward or backward, being propped up by the students in the circle, and then be gently 'passed' around the circle.

> When beginning this activity make sure the circle is very tight (this makes it much easier). As the students get more comfortable they can make the circle slightly bigger. Make sure there is NO talking during this activity and everyone is in a calm/focused state of mind.

- Allow every student a chance to be in the center. This is key for creating a group that feels equally involved and responsible for one another.
- *What did it feel like to rely on someone else? To be responsible for someone else?*

ACTIVITY: Drama Game: Give and Take*
- Divide the class into two groups.
- Have the first group take the stage and form a semi-circle.

- Tell them that after you say *ACTION*, there can only be one person moving (taking) at any given time. Everyone else must be frozen (giving).
- The first person (taker) starts with a movement.
- Once another person starts taking, the current taker must freeze. The taker must continue his/her movement until someone else begins to take.
- The taking should pass randomly throughout the group. There should be no sounds.
- There should be no overlapping taking.
- Tell them that if you as the instructor ever feel that the taking is being dominated by only a few students, or that too much overlapping is happening, you will say "Thank you" which means that group's turn is over and they must sit down.
- Have the next group go up and try the same thing.
- Continue this exercise until you feel the groups are working seamlessly and everyone is taking an equal amount. Make it a competition to see which group can stay up the longest.
- VARIATION:
  - Consider adding sounds in addition to movement.
  - For advanced groups, consider allowing them to have one sound taker and one physical taker at any given time. (i.e. one person must always be making a sound and one person must always be physically moving)
- REFLECTION:
  - *Was it difficult to wait your turn to take? How can this be useful when rehearsing a scene from a play? What skills were required to be successful as a group?*

REFLECTION:

- *In acting it is important that everyone does their share, trusts each other, and works together to create the best possible experience for the audience. Audiences can sense a weak ensemble, and it will ruin their experience of the story.*
- *Think about a time in your life you've been part of a weak ensemble and describe it in your journal. Think about a time in your life you've been part of a strong ensemble and describe it in your journal.*

Lesson 4: Movement & Space (1)

OBJECTIVE: Students will demonstrate the ability to use their whole bodies to convey action and interaction with objects.

MATERIALS: None.

GREETING: None. Jump right into the warm-up...

WARM-UP: What is Pantomime?
- Without any words, gesture for the students to make a seated circle on the stage.
- Gesture to them to begin silently copying (mirroring) your movement.
- Begin a pantomime of your choice (i.e. Waking up in the morning, brushing your teeth, opening the fridge and pouring yourself a bowl of cereal). Be precise and detailed.
- At the end, break the silence and ask the students if they could guess what you were doing.
- *How were you able to guess the activities? What helped you figure it out?*
- *Many times as actors, we have to make the audience believe certain things exist that aren't really there. This is called pantomime.*
- Give an example of poor pantomime, brushing your teeth without clarity.
- *Which paints a better picture, that or what I did previously? In pantomime, every movement should be precise, have a purpose, and help tell the story.*

ACTIVITY: Drama Game: Sound Ball
- Have the students stand in a circle.
- From your pocket, pull out an imaginary ball and introduce it as a *sound ball*.
- *The cool thing about this ball is that the louder the sound you make, the bigger and heavier it gets. The softer the sound you make, the smaller and lighter it gets.*
- Demonstrate growing and shrinking the ball with different sounds.
- Pass the ball around the circle. After each student receives the ball they should make a loud or soft sound to grow it or shrink it, then pass it to their neighbor.
- Encourage the students to put the weight of the ball into their whole body.
- After passing it around once, allow them to bounce the ball across the circle.

> Encourage the kids to not use real words but instead just sounds. If the young kids have trouble with this, they can just say their name to grow and shrink the ball.

> When passing the ball across the circle encourage every student to make eye contact with the intended recipient.

ACTIVITY: Drama Game: Bucket of Water*
- *Now let's experiment with the weight of objects in a real world situation.*
- With the class seated, ask two students to take the stage.
- Ask these two students to together hold a large, imaginary bucket, one person holding each side.
- The instructor will fill the bucket with water from an imaginary hose.
- The goal of the pair of students is to carry the bucket from one side of the stage to the other. Then they are to dump out the water and bring the bucket back.
- The kids should demonstrate the differences in weight between the filled bucket versus the empty bucket using their body and expressions.
- Consider adding other elements to the activity: it's freezing cold, the bucket really smells, the floor is slippery, etc.

ACTIVITY: Drama Game: Tug-of-War*
- *Now let's explore strength and resistance.*
- Have students pair off.
- Ask one pair to take the stage to help demonstrate the game. One at a time, each player will try to pull the other over a designated center line, exactly as you would in regular tug-of-war.
- In this case, however, the rope is not visible but imagined.
- Allows the pairs to play simultaneously, then call up pairs one at a time for observation.
- After the game has been played by several pairs, gradually add more students to both ends of the rope until the entire group is involved.

> Encourage the students to use every part of their body when playing this activity: your feet, your face, your back, your shoulders! Remind them the goal is to make it as believable as possible. Encourage cooperation rather than competition, where successful partners will be the ones that make it the most believable.

REFLECTION:
- *The goal of any pantomime is to make the audience believe something exists that isn't really there. Movement should always be precise, have a purpose, and help tell the story. It should never confuse the audience but instead feel natural and part of the scene.*
- *Think of one character on a TV show or movie that you feel is really good at using their body when acting. Describe that character in your journal.*

Lesson 5: Movement & Space (2)

OBJECTIVE: Students will further demonstrate the ability to use their whole bodies to convey objects and actions, and to understand the difference between activity and action.

MATERIALS: Large writing surface (chart paper, dry erase board)

GREETING: Reflect on previous lesson, share a few journal entries, layout the goal for today.

WARM-UP: Drama Game: 3 Person Tableau
- Create a standing circle.
- One player is to enter the circle and strike a pose that demonstrates some activity (playing baseball, driving a car)
- Two other volunteers enter the circle and strike poses that represent objects that *compliment* the scene of the first player
    - EXAMPLE 1: First Player: a baseball player at bat. Second Player: a pitcher. Third Player: a fanatic fan in the stands.
    - EXAMPLE 2: First Player: someone skiing. Second Player: a tree. Third Player: The snow falling from the sky.
- Once all three players are frozen, that turn has ended and the players go back to the circle. Then a new round starts.

> You can use this opportunity to introduce the idea of a tableau, or frozen picture representing a scene from a story.

> Encourage the students to be as creative as possible when thinking of objects that compliment the scene.

ACTIVITY 1: Drama Game: Ding!
- If you haven't already, discuss "What is Pantomime?" using the activity in the previous lesson.
- Four volunteers are needed: one eye-witness and three detectives trying to solve a murder case.
- The three detectives are sent out of the room beyond hearing range.
- Together the class decides on three clues: 1) a place 2) an occupation of the victim 3) a murder weapon. Write them on the board.
- The first detective is called into the room. Make sure the detective cannot see the board.
- The eye-witness will convey in order what each clue is to the first detective, using only pantomime (no words).
- Once the first detective believes they know what each clue is they say "Ding!" (a lightbulb going off).
- Without saying what they think the clues are, the next detective is called in and now the first detective tries to pantomime to the second detective each clue
- The second detective says "Ding!" for all three clues then pantomimes for the third detective.

14

- Once the third detective knows all three clues he/she says them out loud.
- *Did he get them right?*
- Continue for several rounds.
- *What kind of movements seemed to work the best? Was anything lost in translation?*

ACTIVITY 2: Pantomime Scenes
- Divide the class into groups of 3-4.
- Tell the groups you will give them 10 minutes to create their own short pantomime story.
- Before they rehearse their story, they must write down in their journals the beginning, middle and end of the story.
- Encourage the students in involve every actor, and make the story as clear as possible.
- Have the groups share their scenes.
- Allow the audience to guess what the beginning, middle and end of each scene was.

REFLECTION:
- *Why is exploring pantomime important to becoming a great actor?*
- *In your drama journal write down one scene that you think would be the most difficult scene in the world to pantomime. Make sure it has a beginning, middle and end.*

Lesson 6: "Where"/Environment (I)

OBJECTIVE: Students will explore how to bring environment (where) into play when making acting choices.

MATERIALS: Slips of paper with "where" environments written on them. A birthday party hat.

GREETING: Reflect on previous lesson, share a few journal entries, layout the goal for today.

WARM-UP: Environment Exploration
- In a standing circle, have the students close their eyes and imagine they have been playing in the snow for a very long time.
- *What does it feel like?* Ask them to put that feeling in their whole bodies; their shoulders, faces, backs, hands and toes.
- *Are your feet a little wet? Are your fingers numb? Are you shivering?*
- Tell them a snow storm as just picked up and the snow is lashing at their faces. *Put it in your body.*
- *Finally you walk into a warm cabin. There's a fire burning. You take off your big, damp jacket. Someone hands you a cup of hot chocolate. You start to feel warmth in your whole body as you sit down by the fire.*
- Tell them to open their eyes.
- *What did it feel like going from one environment to another? How did it change your body?*

> *Consider quietly playing instrumental, wintery music to enhance this activity. Or have your music director improvise as you narrate.*

ACTIVITY: Drama Game: Birthday Party Environment
- Divide the class into two groups.
- Tell the first group to take the stage.
- Choose one student to be the birthday boy or girl.
- Explain that they are all at a birthday party, and their goal is to sing "Happy Birthday" to the birthday boy/girl (if you have a birthday hat prop that would help).
- They are going to repeat this scene several times, however before each scene you are going to give them a different environment.
- Their job is to let the environment effect how they act and sing at the birthday party.
- After a few turns, let the other group go.
- Choose a different birthday boy/girl each time.
- REFLECT: *Which environment had the most energy? The least? Which environment felt the happiest?*

> *List of possible environments:*
> - *Library*
> - *Hail storm*
> - *Beach*
> - *Cave*
> - *Forest*
> - *Living Room*
> - *Sewer*
> - *North Pole*
> - *Supermarket*
> - *Hospital*
> - *Airport*
> - *Church*
> - *Desert*
> - *Boat*
> - *The Moon*
> - *Messy Bedroom*
> - *Perfectly Organized Kitchen*
> - *Bus stop*

ACTIVITY: Drama Game: Three Objects*
- Hand out a slip of paper with a "where" environment written on it to every student.
- Their goal is to enter the stage, interact with 3 specific objects in that environment, then exit. (For example, if the environment is "bedroom": Player enters, goes to the closet to pull out a hat, goes to the dresser to put on a belt, then looks at herself in the mirror, then exits. Etc.)
- There should be no talking.
- The class must try to guess what the environment is and what three objects were used.

REFLECTION:
- *What was your favorite type of environment to act in? Why? What was the most difficult?*
- *In your drama journal, write down your favorite place to be. Describe it in detail; the colors, the sounds, the smells, the feeling.*

Lesson 7: "Where"/Environment (2)

OBJECTIVE: Students will explore how to bring environment into play when making acting choices.

MATERIALS: None.

GREETING: Reflect on previous lesson, share a few journal entries, layout the goal for today.

WARM-UP: Drama Game: Two Person Environment
- In a standing circle, give the students 30 seconds to quietly think of a specific environment. (i.e. The circus, a football game, detention, etc.)
- Choose a student to begin by stepping into the circle, instantly beginning to act within the environment he thought of. When the player who was standing to his left in the circle, becomes aware of what the environment is, she steps into the circle and joins the environment. Player 2 then says one line of dialogue to Player 1, Player 1 responds, then the scene is over and they take their place back in the circle.
- EXAMPLE: Player 1 steps into the circle and immediately begins wiping his brow from sweat. Player 2 enters the circle and looks equally hot and exhausted, and tries to pour the last drops of water from her canteen into her mouth. Player 2 says "I don't know how you convinced me to go on this hike through the Sahara Desert." Player 1 says "Well, you said you wanted a vacation in the sun!" Scene is over.
- Repeat in pairs going around the circle.

ACTIVITY: Drama Game: Group Environment
- Divide the class into groups of 4-5.
- Ask the first group to take the stage and assign them an environment (use the list in the previous lesson or create your own). For this example: a kitchen.
- One by one players enter the scene and interact with one object (i.e. a player enters and opens a refrigerator) and exits.
- Each subsequent player that enters must use the object that the players before him created before as well as introduce one new element.
- The last player to enter must remember every thing that was used before him.
- Once the final player has gone, reflect on the environment and have each player say what object they created.
- *Were they consistent the whole time? Did any of the objects happen to move during the scene? Did the objects seem to be consistently the same size/weight?*

ACTIVITY: Drama Game: Where Conversation
- Pair the students up.
- Each pair needs to choose an environment, and an unrelated topic of conversation.

- The goal of each pair is to have a conversation while continuously interacting with their environment in small, specific ways.
- The conversation **must be** completely unrelated to the environment they are in.
- EXAMPLE 1: Two people discussing the latest Harry Potter movie while taking the bus to school. As they chat they stand on the street with their backpacks, they see the bus arrive, they get on the bus, they look for a seat, they find a seat and maybe wave to a few friends, etc.
- EXAMPLE 2: Two friends are playing tennis while discussing the cute boy at school. We see them grabbing balls from the ground, serving, etc. At one point we see one person win the match, and they high-five "good game", all while continuing the conversation.
- Give each pair 5 minutes to rehearse their short scene/conversation.
- Have each pair come up to the stage perform their scene and have the audience guess the environment at the end.
- *Everyday in life we interact with our environment in so many specific ways without even realizing it. The more we can bring this "real world" environment into our acting on stage, the more believable our characters will be.*

REFLECTION
- *Over the next week choose one interesting environment you've visited and describe it in detail in your journal. Describe the colors, the shapes, the smells, the sounds, the overall feel.*

Lesson 8: "Who"/Character Development (I)

OBJECTIVE: Students will demonstrate the ability to understand what makes characters unique and portray different types of characters on stage.

MATERIALS: Slips of paper with different characters written on them (see list to the right).

GREETING: Reflect on previous lesson, share a few journal entries, layout the goal for today.

WARM-UP: Drama Game: Exaggeration Circle
- Players stand in a circle.
- One player starts a small gesture.
- The next player takes it over and makes it even bigger.
- This continues all the way around until the last person takes it to the EXTREME.
- After a few rounds, tell the players they can add a sound as well.
- Encourage the kids to never lose a sense of the original gesture in their exaggerations.
- Explain that a great way to develop characters for the stage is to take take small traits and then enhance them to the extreme.

ACTIVITY: Character Exploration
- *From a distance, could you tell the difference between two school friends and two strangers chatting in park? How?*
- *What are major differences between your mom and your teacher? Your dad and your soccer coach?*
- *In order to effectively tell a story, the audience needs to believe the characters we are trying to play. The better defined the characters, the more the story will resonate and connect with an audience.*

ACTIVITY: Drama Game: Bus Stop
- Create a row of chairs on stage (a bench).
- Three at a time, students will enter the stage, sit and wait for the bus for awhile, then one at a time give up waiting and exit.
- Before each student enters they will draw a character from a bowl.

List of possible characters:
- Teenager listening to music
- A antsy 5 year old
- The President of the United States
- An escaped prisoner
- A pickpocket/thief
- A police officer
- A business man late for an appointment
- A mom with several very large grocery bags
- A rock musician
- A shy 8 year old
- A news reporter
- An 80-year old
- A runaway child
- A football player after losing a game
- A computer geek
- A bratty 7 year old
- An old person who easily forgets things
- A tourist
- A sick person who needs a hospital
- A pop star
- A very wealthy aristocrat
- A nun
- A 12 year old obsessed with games on her iPhone
- A ballerina
- A crazy old person who keeps muttering to herself
- A student studying for an exam
- An alien
- A clown
- A farmer

- The goal is to put that character into every part of their bodies and convey specific behaviors while in the scene.
- After they exit the audience can guess the character of each actor.

ACTIVITY: Drama Game: Status [OPTION 1]
- When characters interact, the principle of *status* always comes into play, whether we're aware of it or not.
- Explain and explore the idea of "status": *The technical definition of status is "the relative social, professional, or other standing of someone." We all have different status in different situations. From now on we will describe it on a 1-10 scale, 10 being practically a God and 1 being the lowliest creature you can imagine. What status are you? If a 10 walked in the room, would you talk to him/her? What about a 1? When was a time in which you were a 10 – in other words, when you had complete power and authority in a situation? How about a 1?*
- Have slips of paper each with a number from 1-10 written on it. Mix them up in a bowl/hat.
- One at a time, students will draw a number from a hat.
- Without telling us their number, the actor enters the stage, stands, and exits as that number.
- Allow the audience to try and guess what number they were.
- After everyone has gone, ask two students to take the stage and improvise a scene. You will assign them the setting and conflict (see list to the right). Assign one student "high" status and the other "low" status.
- Half-way through, tell them to "switch" statuses. Make sure they don't switch characters, but only who is in control of the situation, keeping their original characters and scene.
- REFLECTION:
    - Explain that status is one more layer they can add to their characters.
    - If you are rehearsing a play, ask them to think about each scene their character is in and what "status number" their character would be. What factors are influencing their level of status? Does the status change at any point during the play?

List of possible scenarios:
- *At a dance lesson*
- *Running a marathon*
- *At recess*
- *Studying for a hard test*
- *Filming a movie*
- *Long lost twins meeting after 10 years apart*
- *On a jungle safari*
- *Karate lessons*
- *At a birthday party*
- *Flying a plane*
- *Robbing a bank*
- *On a pirate ship*
- *Visiting the Dentist*
- *Training for a job*
- *Taking a pet to the vet*
- *Visiting the Doctor*
- *Buying a car*
- *Having your hair done at the salon*
- *Visiting someone in hospital*
- *On a spying mission*
- *The first men in space*
- *At a fancy restaurant*
- *Police officer pulls someone over*
- *Looking for buried treasure*
- *Customer complaining to chef about a meal*
- *Two hunters looking for deer*
- *Two criminals on the run*
- *Stuck in a car teetering on the edge of a cliff*
- *Trapped in an elevator*

ACTIVITY: Drama Game: Hitchhiker [OPTION 2 if you feel "Status" is too advanced]
- Place four chairs on stage to represent four seats in a car. Four students start in the car and improvise driving somewhere. They are allowed to talk.
- A "hitchhiker" stands up and puts his/her thumb out. The hitchhiker has a very strong character trait (i.e. enormous sneezes, extremely old age, annoyed business person, etc.)

- One of the passengers will say "look, hitchhiker" and they will pull over to pick the hitchhiker up.
- The hitchhiker enters the front passenger seat and the other students rotate around clockwise. The driver gets out of the car.
- As soon as the hitchhiker enters the car, all the passengers take on the hitchhiker's characteristics immediately and to the extreme.
- They continue dialogue until a new hitchhiker steps into the scene.

REFLECTION:
- *Why do we need interesting characters?*
- *Drama Journal: Over the next week choose one interesting person in your life and describe his/her characteristics in detail.*

Lesson 9: "Who"/Character Development (2)

OBJECTIVE: Students will demonstrate the ability to understand what makes characters unique, and portray 3-dimensional characters on stage.

MATERIALS: Copies of the Facebook Character Development Worksheet (on next page) for each student.

GREETING: Reflect on previous lesson, share a few journal entries, layout the goal for today.

WARM-UP: Drama Game: Human Barometer
- Tell the students to spread out on stage.
- Tell them that they are going to be a human barometer.
- As you ask questions, they're going to decide how much they agree or disagree.
- Stage Right is agree 100%, Stage Left is disagree 100%. They can be anywhere in between. Encourage the students to be as truthful as they can.
- Check out the list to the right for suggested statements.
- Bring them together for a short reflection.
- *What did you notice? Is everyone in this room very similar in regards to their likes and dislikes? Was there a big range?*
- NOTE: If rehearsing a play, this is a great game to play having the students act and think as their characters instead of themselves.

> List of possible statements:
> - Breakfast is the best meal of the day
> - Math is my favorite class
> - I like pineapples
> - I get scared very easily
> - I'd like to be famous one day
> - I like sports
> - Stealing is wrong
> - I'd like to live in another country
> - [_____] is the best drama teacher ever :)
> - I like the rain
> - I watch TV every night

ACTIVITY: Character Discussion
- *There are hundreds of ingredients that go into making somebody the person they are. Their background, family, hobbies, their likes and dislikes, their fears, their hopes, their dreams, their environment. The more depth we can show when playing characters on stage, the more interesting and relatable the story will be.*

ACTIVITY: Character Facebook Profile
- *We're going to develop our own characters.* (If you are rehearsing a play, this activity can be used for the kids to develop the characters they've been cast as.)
- Give every kid a copy of the Facebook Character Development Worksheet (on the next page)
- *Nowadays we put our entire personal lives on social media, so we're going to use a Facebook profile as a tool for building a well-rounded character.*
- Give them 10-15 minutes to fill out the form creating a brand new character from scratch. Encourage them to be adventurous, but believable.

- Have the students get on stage and walk around as their characters.
- Every so often say freeze, approach a character and ask him/her a question. Let the class listen, then continue walking.

> Consider playing some music as they walk around, or call our different environments.

ACTIVITY: Character Improv
- Using the characters they just developed, ask students two at a time to take the stage.
- Give them a specific setting/situation (you can use the list provided in the previous lesson)
- They are to improvise a short scene as their characters.
- Encourage them to be bold and honest.

REFLECTION:
- *How did filling out the Facebook profile affect your portrayal of the character?*
- *Did it make it easier or harder?*
- *In your journal make a list of five characters you are drawn to in either books, TV or film. Describe why.*

acebook Home Profile Friends Inbox (1)   Settings   Log out

Username: _____   5 minutes ago

| Wall | Info | Photos | + |

[profile pic]

View photos of me (34)

nformation
elationship Status:
urrent City:
rthday:

riends

Basic information
Age:
Gender:
Place of Birth:
Hair Color:
Eye Color:
Height:

Personal Information
Hobbies/Interests:

Favorite Music:

Favorite Movie:

Your biggest dream:

Your biggest fear:

Someone you look up to:

Your deepest secret:

Your best friend:

If you had a day to do whatever you could, what would you do?

Education and Work
Current Job:

Past Jobs:

Do you like or dislike your job? Why?

Education:

Groups
Member of:

Lesson 10: "Why"/Objective & Tactics

OBJECTIVE: Students will explore the idea of objective and tactics, and how they are crucial to acting on stage.

MATERIALS: Candy bar.

GREETING: Reflect on previous lesson, share a few journal entries, layout the goal for today.

WARM-UP: Who wants this candy bar?
- After the kids have settled in pull out a candy bar.
- Tell them: *Someone just gave this candy bar before class and I don't really like them, who wants this?*
- Most likely chaos will ensue at this point. Let it. Egg them on with: *Hm, I don't know, not sure who I should give it to...* Point out a few individual students. *Jamie, do you want it? Why should I give it to you? Gabby, what would you do for it?*
- Finally, choose one student to give it to.

EXPLORATION: Objective & Tactics
- *Why did everyone act the way they just did? Because you wanted something - in other words, you had an objective.*
- *The game we just played was an example of setting an objective.*
- *Objectives are what we want and tactics are how we try to get it.* Turn this phrase into a rap and have the class repeat it with you several times.
- *Imagine watching a movie where none of the characters wanted anything at all. The characters just wandered around, aimlessly. Pretty boring, right?*
- *It's important for characters to have objectives because it's what moves the story along and keeps it interesting.*
- Give every student 30 seconds to think of one thing they did today before class, and how it connects to a certain *want*. (For example: This morning I ate a bowl of cereal, because I *wanted* to avoid feeling hungry and having my stomach growl in class.)
- Go around the circle allowing everyone to share.

Feel free to jump in and help out younger students if necessary.

ACTIVITY: Drama Game: Smile!
- Set out chairs in a large circle, facing inward.
- When students arrive have them sit down.
- Ask for one volunteer to come to the middle.
- Explain that the goal of the person in the middle is to make one of the students in the circle smile.

- They can use any method they want without touching anyone.
- If the person in the middle gets another student to smile, that student trades places and the game continues.
- The objective of the person in the middle is to get someone to smile, the objective of all the players sitting is to keep a straight face.

ACTIVITY: Create a Scene
- In pairs, students must come up with their own two-person scenes.
- Each scene must have someone with a clear objective, and 3 different tactics to acheive that objective. The first 2 tactics should fail, while the 3rd tactic succeeds.
- Give the pairs 10 minutes to rehearse this.
- Let the students share.
- Ask the audience if they can identify the objectives and tactics.

REFLECTION:
- *Observe your family tonight and write down three objectives you saw them working towards. Then write down one tactic they used. Did it work?*

Lesson 11: Focus/Concentration

OBJECTIVE: Students will practice the skill of staying focused, and understand how staying "in character" and serving the story is the most important thing to remember on stage.

MATERIALS: None.

WARM-UP: Group Count
- Actors stand in circle and look at the floor.
- The goal is for the group to count from 1 to 10.
- Any actor will start by saying "1"
- Any other actor will continue by saying "2" and so on until you reach "10".
- If any two players say a number at the same time the group must start again at "1".
- *What helped to make this activity successful?*
- *Did it help or hurt the process when after a mistake everyone call out "Brian, c'mon! Gosh!"*

EXPLORATION: Focus
- *The games we're working on today challenge us to concentrate and focus, regardless of what may be happening around us. Audience members can immediately detect an actor that breaks focus. It can disconnect the audience from the story taking place on stage. As actors we always strive to stay in our characters and in the story.*

ACTIVITY: Drama Game: Pass the Sound
- *We're going to begin by working on concentration, and later we'll use that concentration to stay in character on stage.*
- In a standing circle, pass a "whoosh" around the circle. This is done by saying "whoosh!" and throwing your hands toward the person next to you.
- After is goes around a couple times stop the "Whoosh!" and send a "Bing!" going the opposite way, using a different hand gesture.
- Now tell the kids they need to put their focus caps on, because you're going to send a "Whoosh!" going one direction, then a "Bing!" going the opposite direction. At some point they of course will overlap over one student so that student needs to be prepared.
- Try this out a few times.
- If they're up for it, try adding in a 3rd layer, "Ooga!".
- *Was this easy or difficult? What made it hard? If it crossed over you, what did you have to do to keep the game going?*
- *On stage we have to do our best, especially when all eyes are on us and we're feeling nervous, to keep the story going.*

ACTIVITY: Drama Game: "Sausage"
- *Let's practice using focus to help us "stay in character" on stage.*
- Divide the class into two groups, Group A and Group B.
- Have Group A form a single file line offstage right, and Group B form a single file line offstage left.
- One person from Group A and Group B will walk toward the center.
- "A" will face "B" and ask him/her a question. No matter the question, "B" must keep a straight face and answer "sausage".
- Then they will exit and a new pair will take the stage.
- EXAMPLE:
  - A: What's that hanging from your ear? B: Sausage.
  - A: What's your sister's name? B: Sausage
  - A: How old are you? B: Sausage.
- After everyone has gone, select a few volunteers to go into the "hot seat" and ask him/her several rapid fire questions, in which each response should be "sausage" with a straight face. See if they can get through 8 questions in a row.

> *This game is usually a big hit with kids. The more it's played, the better the students will get at keeping their focus when funny things happen on stage.*

ACTIVITY: Drama Game: 3-way Conversation*
- *This last game will challenge you to keep your concentration when you're being pulled in many different directions.*
- Place three chairs in a row on the stage facing the audience.
- Ask for three volunteers to sit in each chair.
- The players on the left and right are to think of conversations they will have with the player in the middle.
- When you say "action", it is the goal of the middle player to be able to keep two conversations going at the same time, with the players to his left and right. The outside players should only acknowledge the middle player.
- When you say "shift", the player stage right should exit while the other two players shift over. A new player should take the spot stage left and the activity begins again.

> *Encourage the outside players to leave a little bit of space in their conversations to allow the middle player to manage. The conversations should be completely unrelated.*

REFLECTION:
- *Why is focus so important?*
- *In your journal, write down two ways you could help yourself and your castmates stay focused when performing in front of an audience.*

Lesson 12: Utilizing Voice (1)

OBJECTIVE: Students will demonstrate the understanding of how projection, articulation and voice variation are necessary parts to being a strong actor.

MATERIALS: List of tongue twisters (attached on the next page).

GREETING:
- In a very quiet, barely audible and inarticulate voice welcome the students to class. Briefly chat about the previous session and what the goal is for today (the kids should be confused and really struggling to hear).
- Without any gestures, tell them to take the stage and create a circle. When they don't do it, start to get frustrated and ask again. Get more frustrated and call out specific students.
- Finally, in your regular voice, smile and ask them:
- *Why didn't you do what I asked?*
- *What was frustrating about not being able to hear?*
- *What could I have improved to make you understand me better?*

EXPLORATION: Voice
- *Today we're focusing on our voice. Making sure the audience hears every world is crucial to helping them understand the story. Projection, articulation and exaggeration are all tools that will help us achieve this goal.* Write the words "Projection", "Articulation" and "Exaggeration" up on the board and have students help you define them.

ACTIVITY: Vocal Warm-Up
- *In order to speak clearly it helps to warm up our voices.*
- Tell the kids to make their faces as big as they can for 5 seconds.
- Then tell them to make make their faces as tiny as they can for 5 seconds.
- Tell them to stand up tall, pull their shoulders back and relax them, put their hands on their stomachs, take a big breathe in then say "Ha! Ha! Ha!". They should feel their bellies bouncing.
- *This is where the strength of our voice comes from.* Practice a few times.
- Say the following commands loudly and precisely: *Repeat after me: "Articulate!" (Articulate!) "Exaggerate!" (Exaggerate!) "Project your voice!" (Project your voice!)* Repeat.

> Exaggeration Phrases:
> - Unique New York
> - World wide web
> - I was born on a pirate ship
> - The lips, the teeth, the top of the tongue
> - A horse, a horse, my kingdom for a horse

ACTIVITY: Drama Game: Vocal Exaggeration Circle
- *Let's focus on exaggeration.*
- Have the students make a standing circle.
- Choose a phrase from the column to the right (simple tongue twisters) and have the kids choose an emotion.

30

- Each player is going to say this phrase going around the circle, however it's going to get more and more exaggerated as it progresses.
- For each new phrase start at a different part of the circle.

ACTIVITY: Drama Game: Tongue Twisters
- Introduce a tongue twister to the class, and have a short competition to see who can say it the most times without messing up.
- Hand out the tongue twisters list to each student and tell them they must pick one tongue twister and think of one emotion.
- Give them a few minutes to practice.
- One by one have each student take the stage, stand firmly in the center and say his/her tongue twister with excellent projection, articulation and exaggeration.

ACTIVITY: Drama Game: Group Story with Characters

By dividing the class into two groups, half the class will always be able to learn from observing.

- Divide the class into two groups.
- Group one will take the stage, create a semi-circle and make up a story one sentence at a time.
- The first person to begin must make a very strong character choice in his/her voice that everyone else must imitate.
- If at any point a player in the group loses the character or speaks too softly or doesn't articulate, say "NEXT", which means the next group takes the stage to begin a brand new story with a brand new character.
- Make it a competition to see which group can last the longest.

REFLECTION:
- *In your journal make a list of three other occupations where you feel articulation is extremely important. Why?*

List of Tongue Twisters

- Unique New York
- Three free throws
- Red Leather, Yellow Leather
- I thought a thought
  But the thought I thought wasn't the thought I thought I thought
- One-One was a racehorse
  Two-Two was one, too
  When One-One won one race
  Two-Two won one, too
- Say this sharply, say this sweetly
  Say this shortly, say this softly
  Say this sixteen times very quickly
- Rubber Baby Buggy Bumpers!
- Silly Sally swiftly shooed seven silly sheep
  The seven silly sheep Silly Sally shooed
  Shilly-shallied south
- These sheep shouldn't sleep in a shack
  Sheep should sleep in a shed.
- Red Bulb Blue Bulb Red Bulb Blue Bulb
- Red Blood Blue Blood
- I wish to wish the wish you wish to wish, but if you wish the wish the witch wishes, I won't wish the wish you wish to wish
- She sells seashells on the seashore
- Mix a box of mixed biscuits with a boxed biscuit mixer
- A proper copper coffee pot
- Toy boat. Toy boat. Toy boat.
- Betty bought butter but the butter was bitter, so Betty bought better butter to make the bitter butter better

- If the thought I thought I thought had been the thought I thought, I wouldn't have thought so much
- How much wood could a wood chuck; chuck if a wood chuck could chuck wood
- Comical economists
- Which wristwatches are Swiss wristwatches?
- Peter Piper picked a peck of pickled peppers
  A peck of pickled peppers Peter Piper picked
  If Peter Piper picked a peck of pickled peppers
  Where's the peck of pickled peppers Peter Piper picked?
- Sasha sews slightly slashed sheets shut
- She should shun the shinning sun
- The big black back brake broke badly
- The big beautiful blue balloon burst
- A shapeless sash sags slowly
- Smelly shoes and socks shock sisters
- Dick kicks sticky bricks
- Shave a single shingle thin
- Stick strictly six sticks stumps
- Cinnamon aluminum linoleum
- New York is unanimously universally unique
- Cooks cook cupcakes quickly
- Flora's freshly fried fish
- A bragging baker baked black bread
- Buy blue blueberry biscuits before bedtime
- She sold six shabby sheared sheep on ship
- The sixth sick sheik's son slept
- These thousand tricky tongue twisters trip thrillingly off the tongue

Lesson 13: Utilizing Voice (2)

OBJECTIVE: Students will learn to communicate with their voice without using words, instead focusing on tone, rhythm and pitch.

MATERIALS: None.

GREETING/WARM-UP:
- Begin the class by talking in gibberish.
- Communicate the following without actually saying any words, only sounds (gestures are fine):
- *Welcome, class! I'm so excited to see you today. You see, I was very frustrated early this morning because when I tried to leave my house my car wouldn't start. I had to call a mechanic to come fix it and it took sooooo long for him to arrive. But he finally showed up, fixed it, but then as I was driving here I got pulled over by a cop! He said I was driving too fast! I tried to explain that I was late for class. Fortunately he was very nice and let me go. Thanks goodness! Now I'm finally here and glad that whole mess is over. Whew. Anyway, let's begin. Would you please come join me in a circle?*
- When they join the circle you can stop speaking in gibberish and ask them the following questions:
- *Who understood what I was saying earlier?*
- *How did you know? What did I do that helped communicate what was happening to me?*
- *Gibberish means speaking with silly sounds that don't mean anything, but still communicate an intention and meaning.*
- *Speaking in gibberish helps us concentrate on using the "sound" and "quality" of our voice as opposed to words.*

WARM-UP:
- Give the students 1 minute to turn to their neighbor and have a conversation in gibberish.
- *Now let's tell a group story, one sentence at a time, in gibberish. Try to be precise as you can with your descriptions.*

ACTIVITY: Drama Game: Gibberish Interpreter*
- Ask two students to take the stage.
- One will speak gibberish, and the other will translate the gibberish into English.
- Give the gibberish student a specific situation to talk about, or take suggestions from the class. (i.e. You have just won the world's biggest hot dog eating contest and are telling us all about it.)
- The gibberish speaker should speak only one line at a time, using

OTHER SCENARIOS:
-A scientist explaining her recent discovery of a 2nd moon
- A pop singer giving a press conference after falling asleep during his concert performance
- A child describing what it was like getting her first cavity
- A chef explaining how to cook his favorite meal, candy spaghetti (or anything else!)
- A farmer explaining how to milk a cow in record time

as much physicality as he/she can.
- Then the interpreter will mimic the motions and translate the phrase into English.
- Encourage the gibberish speaker to be very specific in his/her intention and actions.
- Encourage the interpreter to think very carefully about trying to make the gibberish make sense.
- After awhile, allow the class to act as the "press" and ask questions.

ACTIVITY: Drama Game: Gibberish Conversation*
- Ask two students to take the stage. They will be the actors in the scene.
- Ask two more students to stand on either side of them. They will be the interpreters.
- Give the actors a topic. (Or ask for a suggestion from the class.)
- The first actor speaks a line in gibberish, then his interpreter will translate it into english for the audience.
- The second actor then responds in gibberish, while her interpreter translates.
- EXAMPLE:
  - Topic: Laundry
  - Actor 1: *Gil frelic neber seber trolli?*
  - Interpreter 1: *Is that pleasant smell coming from you?*
  - Actor 2: *Poy yoy, beek ploter woter magory.*
  - Interpreter 2: *Why yes, last night I washed my clothes in my dad's cologne.*
  - Etc.

> OTHER TOPIC IDEAS:
> - Lunch
> - Cowboy
> - Math
> - iPhone
> - Swimming
> - Mars
> - Disneyland
> - Cooking
> - Jealousy
> - Armpit
> - Justin Bieber

> Another option, if you have more time, is to break the class up into groups of 4. Each group will have 2 gibberish speakers and 2 interpreters. They have 5 minutes to create a scene with a beginning, middle and end, then share it with the class.

REFLECTION:
- What did it feel like not being able to use words?
- What other skills did you have to rely on?
- How could you apply those skills to your regular acting?
- This week in your journal create an imaginary character with a speaking voice unlike anything you've heard before. Go extreme. Describe the character (or even better fill out a Facebook Character Profile) and write a 3 sentence monologue for him/her.

Lesson 14: Listening/Reacting

OBJECTIVE: Students will understand how listening and reacting to events in a scene can be just as important as speaking.

MATERIALS: A prop phone.

GREETING: Reflect on previous lesson, share a few journal entries, layout the goal for today.

WARM-UP: Bippity Bippity Bop
- The entire class stands in a circle and the teacher stands in the middle of the circle.
- LEVEL 1: The teacher points at someone in the circle and says "bippity bippity bop" as fast as she can. The person being pointed at must say "bop" before she gets to the end of her phrase. If the teacher points to a student and only says "bop", then the student must stay quiet and not say anything. The goal of the teacher is it get the students to not say "bop" fast enough in the first case scenario, and to say "bop" in the second.
- LEVEL 2: After this level is well understood by the whole group, it is time to add another dimension. If the teacher points to a student and says "haunted house", the student must crouch down and in a ghoulish voice say "Come in! Come in!". The two students to his left and right must use both their arms to make the roof of a house over the crouched student.
- LEVEL 3: If the teacher points to a student and says "Hawaii", the student being pointed at would have todo the hula while the students on the left and right would put their arms up like palm trees.
- If you have time, you can add more in. (Check out our blog post for more ideas.)
- Finally, once the class gets the hang of it, you can add an "elimination mode": if a student messes up, he/she must sit down. Go until you have a winner.

> WARNING: Your kids will LOVE this game. Be prepared to have them ask for it every day after you introduce it. :)

EXPLORATION: Listening & Reacting
- Share something with the kids to get a big reaction out of them.
- EXAMPLE: *I've got some awesome news. I won a contest this morning from Dominos and they're going to deliver 5 free pepperoni pizzas to class in about 15 minutes!*
- Let them react. Then: *Sorry, I was just kidding. There's no contest, and no pizza.*
- Let them react. *But there is a lesson, and it's in what you guys did right now. Your reaction. In life we listen and we react, naturally.*
- *One of the challenges of being an actor is listening and reacting as if you're experiencing events for the first time, even though you've rehearsed the scenes many times before.*

ACTIVITY: Drama Game: TV Reaction

- Divide the class into groups of 3.
- Each group will get 1 minute to choose a show on TV.
- With three chairs placed on stage facing the audience, one at a time each group will sit and watch the TV program they chose. There can be no words. The goal is for them to react together to the events occurring on the program.
- After each group finishes the audience can guess the program they were watching.
- *Did they react together? Did you believe they were watching the same program together?*

ACTIVITY: Drama Game: The Phone Rings
- Divide the class in half. Ask the first half to stand in a line offstage.
- Place a prop phone on a stool center stage.
- One at a time the students are to enter as if the phone is ringing, pick it up, and listen to the voice on the other line.
- Over the course of 30 seconds they are to silently react to the voice on the other line by going from one emotion, to the exact opposite, then back to the first. They should strive to be as believable as possible.
- The moment after they pick up the phone you will tell them who is on the other line, then there will be only silence as they imagine the rest of the conversation in their head.
- EXAMPLE:
    - Player 1 walks on stage.
    - She picks up the phone.
    - The instructor says "Your best friend asking to go to the park."
    - Player 1 shows excitement while continuing to listen to the conversation, then something happens in the conversation that makes her gradually show sadness or concern, then finally back to excitement.
    - The whole time is should seem like there is someone on the other line.

> PHONE IDEAS:
> - Your mean principal
> - Your dad saying he's bringing home pizza
> - Your brother asking for help
> - A doctor with bad news
> - You've won the lottery
> - Your soccer coach telling you practice is cancelled
> - Your grandma
> - Your weird cousin
> - Your piano teacher reminding you to practice
> - Your crush
> - Your best friend telling you a secret
> - Etc.

ACTIVITY: Drama Game: Twin Interview
- Group the students into different groups of three.
- Each group should choose one person to act as the interviewer, while the other two have to answer as "twins".
- After the interviewer asks a questions, the twins must answer in sync with each other, without discussing the answer between them. They have to listen to each other and react/speak at the same time with the same words to answer the question.
- Give the groups a few minutes to practice.
- Ask for a volunteer twin group to take the stage. Have the class (and you) ask them questions one at a time.

36

- Allow several different volunteer twins to have a chance.
- After awhile, try moving on to do the same exercise with "twin" groups of at least five, using the same principles, allowing the whole group to respond to questions as a single person.

REFLECTION:
- *What did you discover through these reacting and listening activities?*
- In your journal think of someone you know who generally has big, expressive reactions to things and someone you know who has more subdued reactions to things. Describe how and if it affects how you speak to them.

Lesson 15: Stage Directions/Blocking

OBJECTIVE: Students will demonstrate an understanding of stage directions, the principles of blocking, and how to effectively stage a scene.

MATERIALS: Large writing surface.

GREETING: Reflect on previous lesson, share a few journal entries, layout the goal for today.

WARM-UP: Drama Game: Stage Directions
- Briefly discuss with the students stage history and layout: Hundreds of years ago, stages were raked, which means the back of the stage was higher than the front. Since the audiences' seats were usually on a flat level, the stage was raked so that everyone could see the actors more easily.
- Draw a stage on the board.
- With the previous information in mind…have students guess what each area of the stage was called (i.e. Upstage, Downstage, Center Stage, Stage Right, and Stage Left).
- Explain that the directions are always from the ACTOR'S point of view.
- Label each area as the students name them correctly.
- Ask a volunteer to come to the front of the classroom.
- Have the volunteer face the other students (call them the audience).
- Now, ask the student to take one step to Stage Left. If correct, ask student to step back to Center Stage and repeat this process with all of the directions.
- Ask more volunteers to take the stage, making the directions come quicker and quicker.
- Invite the whole class to the stage. Give them the same exercise.
- Now throw in an emotion or activity. (i.e. Saunter downstage left as if your goldfish just died. Skip upstage as if you just received straight A's. etc.)
- Below is a chart that may be helpful for reference:

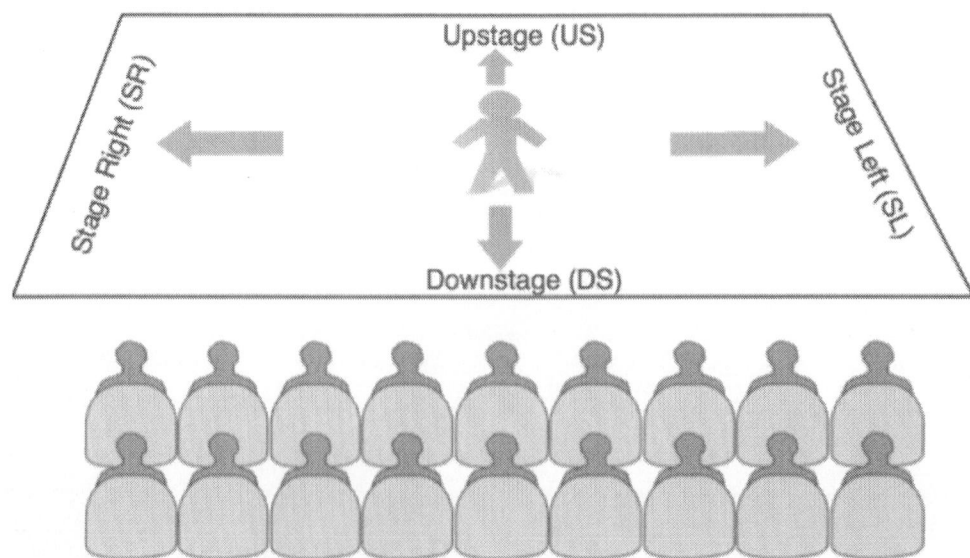

EXPLORATION: Principles of Blocking

- *Where we stand on stage, or "blocking", helps communicate to the audience important information about the story.*
- *Just like in the movies where there is often a blurred background with a focused foreground, our staging can help tell the audience where to focus.*
- *There are three principles of blocking you must always be aware of.*
- Write the three principles on the board one by one and ask the students why they think each one is important
    - **1) Always be open:** *The audience wants to see you, especially when you're speaking. Always try to have your shoulders angled toward the audience so they can see you and hear you. This is called "cheating" toward the audience.*
    - **2) Never a straight line:** *In life we don't stand in straight lines unless we're told to. So on stage we should never make a straight line because it looks fake.*
    - **3) Create depth and height whenever possible:** *Layers make the scene more interesting to look at and feel more natural.*

ACTIVITY: Model a Tableau

- Remind the students of what a "tableau" is: a frozen picture representing a scene from a story.
- Choose 10 students to take the stage.
- Tell them you're going to give them a scene and they have 5 seconds to create a tableau being aware of the 3 principles of blocking.
- Tell them: *In line for an American Idol audition. 5...4...3...2...1...Freeze!*
- Ask the audience how they did. Are they cheating out? Are there levels?
- Make adjustments as needed. Some kids could be sitting on the group listening to music, other kids anxiously standing tall, some in conversation bent over, etc. A "line" doesn't have to be boring.
- Ask another group of 10 to come up and give them another scene: *A playground at recess.*
- Make adjustments as needed.

ACTIVITY: Drama Game: Group Tableau

- Break the class into groups of approximately 6-8 students.
- Each group will be given an event, and their job is to create 3 tableaus that highlight the event: a beginning, a middle, and an end.
- Give the groups 5 minutes to work on it.
- Have each group share. Allow the audience to guess the event. *Was it clear what the event was? Did they obey the principles of blocking? Are there any adjustments you could recommend?*

> Scene Suggestions:
> - Robbing a bank
> - Climbing Mt. Everest
> - Auditioning for a Broadway show
> - Capturing a criminal
> - A surprise birthday party

> Encourage the students to speak in professional stage terms when giving suggestions: "It looks a little crowded upstage left so I think maybe Jon and Abby should move downstage."

REFLECTION:
- *Why is staging important to telling the story?*
- *What are the three principles of blocking?*
- *In your journal draw a picture of 3 empty stages. Choose an event that involves at least 6 people. Sketch out tableaus for the beginning, middle and end of the scene.*

Lesson 16: Putting it All Together

OBJECTIVE: Students will perform and evaluate scenes using the tools they've acquired throughout the semester.

MATERIALS: Scene observation sheets for each student (attached on the next page).

GREETING: Reflect on previous lesson, share a few journal entries, and explain to the class that today they are going to be practicing all the skills they've learned so far.

WARM-UP:
- Warm-up with whichever fun activity yours kids have been requesting or enjoyed the most during the semester. (Bippity Bippity Bop is a great choice).
- The goal here is to loosen everyone up and get the students focused.

EXPLORATION: Observation Sheet
- Hand out the character observation sheets to the students.
- Together go through and discuss each category. They can fill out a score from 1-10 in each category.
- *You will be observing each other during this session based on the criteria in this scene observation sheet.*

ACTIVITY: Scene Creation
- Assign every student a scene partner. It's best to have this pre-determined before class starts. Pair students together who will compliment each other and don't normally work together.
- Each pairing will receive a scenario. You can have these scenarios written on slips of paper in a bowl to be chosen randomly, or you can pre-determine which pairs will be receiving each scenario. Use your best judgement.
- Give the scene partners 5 minutes to discuss and decide what the beginning, middle and end of their scene will be. This must be written down in their notebooks.
- Then give the students 15 minutes to rehearse their scene. While they are rehearsing they should be trying to incorporate all the items on the observation sheet. The scenes are to be no longer than 3 minutes.

ACTIVITY: Scene Sharing/Observation
- Allow each pair a chance to present their scene.
- After each scene give the audience a minute to fill out their observation sheet.
- Ask for a few comments from the audience about what they really liked.
- Give your own personal feedback, first positive, then a constructive critique if needed.
- Continue to go through every scene.

REFLECTION
- *What are some things you learned about acting that you didn't know before this class?*
- *What parts did you find more challenging?*
- *What parts did you find the easiest?*
- *Which activities did you enjoy the most?*
- *Do you feel you have a better understanding of how to effectively tell stories on stage?*
- *In your journal, write a short letter to someone who is interested in acting but has never acted before. Share a bit of your experience.*

SCENE OBSERVATION SHEET

Beat by Beat Press | www.bbbpress.com

	Scene 1:	Scene 2:	Scene 3:
Character Development How well-defined and real did the characters seem?	__/10	__/10	__/10
Movement & Pantomime Did their movement and physicality seem natural and enhance the story?	__/10	__/10	__/10
Objective & Tactics How well defined were the objectives of the characters? Were they consistent?	__/10	__/10	__/10
Voice Did the actors project, use good diction and vocal variation?	__/10	__/10	__/10
Listening & Reacting Were actors connected to the scene even when they weren't speaking?	__/10	__/10	__/10
Blocking Did the blocking enhance the story? Were the actors obeying the 3 principles?	__/10	__/10	__/10
Other			

	Scene 4:	Scene 5:	Scene 6:
Character Development How well-defined and real did the characters seem?	__/10	__/10	__/10
Movement & Pantomime Did their movement and physicality seem natural and enhance the story?	__/10	__/10	__/10
Objective & Tactics How well defined were the objectives of the characters? Were they consistent?	__/10	__/10	__/10
Voice Did the actors project, use good diction and vocal variation?	__/10	__/10	__/10
Listening & Reacting Were actors connected to the scene even when they weren't speaking?	__/10	__/10	__/10
Blocking Did the blocking enhance the story? Were the actors obeying the 3 principles?	__/10	__/10	__/10
Other			

Printed in Great Britain
by Amazon